THE VOICES
OF VIETNAM

VETERANS
SPEAKING OUT

ANELDA ATTAWAY
JEAN A. GLOVER-SCOTT

The Voices of Vietnam, Veterans Speaking Out

Author: Anelda L. Attaway

Visionary: Jean A. Glover-Scott

Cover Created & Designed/Images: Jazzy Kitty Publications

Cover Vision: Anelda Attaway

Interior Images: Submitted from Vietnam Vets

Logo Designs: Andre M. Saunders//Jess Zimmerman

Editor: Anelda L. Attaway

© 2020 Anelda L. Attaway

ISBN 978-1-7357874-4-2

Library of Congress Control Number: Ordered 2020921234

ACKNOWLEDGMENTS

First and foremost, we thank God for giving Jean this vision to have Vietnam Veterans tell their stories from their own words and experiences during the Vietnam War. We appreciate their service.

A special thank you to all of the participants in this book; we couldn't have done it without them. Thank you, Aaron Douglas, Ira Kirch, Rocky L. Hammond Sr., Ira Kirch, John Langjahr, Joel McCormick, Debra McNeely for the Late Hazell Henry McNeely aka Winks, Jean A. Glover-Scott for The Late Cleveland Scott Jr. aka Big Bo, Phillip Ward (Angie daughter), and Harold Richard Williams.

Thank you, Robert H. Carr, William M. Cottingham "Cotton," Jerry Flowers Sr., Sgt. Earnest Hill, and 1st Sgt. EB Charles Porter for allowing us to add you to the book.

Bro. Aaron, Douglas, President Pilgrim Baptist Church, Veterans Ministry; Bro. Aaron Douglas helps the Vietnam Veterans and all the other branches. Your ministry is a blessing to many lives.

Thank you, Kenneth J. Butler, SGT, Retired, MBA, BBA, SME for your participation.

DEDICATIONS

This book is dedicated to my late husband, Cleveland Scott Jr. who served his country in the Vietnam War. He sadly departed this earth on February 22, 2018, at the age of 70 from CJD (Creutzfeldt-Jakob Disease), which my family and I believe came from Agent Orange. I know that Agent Orange and other herbicides were spread over there, and all the soldiers were somehow affected.

Scott,

You always were the leader in our family. All I can say is we built together five children and during all the storms of life, you and I made it through. When I look back over our lives, it's been good times and bad. And no matter what, I know that grace and mercy brought us through because God was always in it all.

Thank you for serving our country. I am grateful that you made it home because so many men lost their lives in Vietnam. When the war was over and the soldiers came back home, they had so many problems. I was told if any soldier was in Vietnam for even 10 minutes, it was the Agent Orange that caused their problems. Therefore, I know in my heart that Agent Orange is the reason you're no longer with us. Scott, I miss you and thank you for your service.

Rest-in-Peace

Ps. My favorite saying is, "God got me!"

With All My Love

Your Wife, Jean A. Glover-Scott

Cleveland Scott Jr. is my oldest son of seven children. Bo, as we so lovingly called him, was intelligent, strong, and definitely a leader.

He was a dedicated worker that loved his family. Also, he was a spiritual man that loved God. Prayer and reading the Bible was of the utmost importance to him. I love and miss my son, dearly.

Rest Well, My Son,

Your Mom, Ellen Scott

Daddy,

We spoke a lot about your time in Vietnam. Thank you for your service. I am just thankful for your safe return home.

You took excellent care of me; I will always cherish my childhood. One of my favorite memories is every year you made Christmas special. There are no words to express how much you are truly missed. Your death has left a huge place in my heart that only you can fill. We had such a special bond that no one could break. Daddy, you loved me in a special way. I knew I could always depend on you. Thank you for the time we have shared on this side. Your diagnosis of CJD is still devastating to me. Truthfully, I can't believe you are gone. But, I hated seeing you suffer because you did not deserve that. That is the only peace I have is knowing that you are resting in peace. And that your spirit is always with me.

Most importantly, I am proud that I was part of your decision to accept Christ as your personal Savior and because of that I know I will see you again; until then, you will be dearly missed.

I Will Love You Forever, Anelda aka Kitten

Daddy aka Papi,

Thank you for your service not just to this country, but to all who had the pleasure of knowing you.

Since you left, life has not been the same. I have been struggling with how your life ended and questioned God about how He could allow this to happen. How could you contract a rare disease that only one out of a million people are stricken with? A disease that would let you leave this earth in just two months of being diagnosed. The answer was so very clear and a soft voice said, *"I had to find someone who was also one in a million and would continue to have faith until the end."*

Papi the pain that I feel as I write this dedication is unbearable. I often think about the many phone calls I would receive from you checking on me, just to see how I was doing. And you would never hang up without telling me that you love me. Your love was a true example of a father's love. My heart aches, knowing that I will never hear the words again. However, I am grateful to have been told by such a loving, awesome, and wonderful father. There is nothing left other than to say THANK YOU, PAPI, for who you were and the character you not only displayed as a father, but as a man. Continue to rest well, PAPI and I will continue to honor you for all the days of my life.

Love you,

Larenda Francis aka Dimples

To My Father,

I miss you and love you very much each and every day. Words can't express how much you meant and how much you had a positive impact on my life as well as my children's lives. You were a father figure to them when they needed it the most and number one, you show me what unconditional love is truly looks like. I appreciate all you've done for our family to be a true leader, father, husband, and friend to many who love you dearly and looked at you as their father. You are one person who would do anything for anybody at any given time, never selfish, always giving of yourself.

Love,

Sharnika aka Nika

My name is Cleveland Scott III, named after my dad. He called me Lil' Bo and he was Big Bo. I was the only son that my parents had. My dad was a strong man that I looked up to. My sister's and I used to tease him that he was Mr. K.I.A. (Know It All). He knew everything; no matter what I asked him, he had an answer. My dad was very supportive and I appreciate him. Since we lost you, I have been looking out for my mom. I hope that you are proud of me. Dad, you are dearly missed.

Love Your Son,

Cleveland Scott III aka Lil Bo

Daddy,

Thank you for teaching me about the Lord and to keep Him first in all things. You have taught me many valuable lessons that I still use to this day! I miss all the advice you gave from everyday life to outfit choices. Thank you for being a wonderful example of what a man should be. You set the bar very high. I will always strive to make you proud of whatever I do. You will be forever missed and forever in my heart.

Love Always Your Favorite and Baby Girl
Marquita aka Keita

Cleveland Scott Jr., my oldest brother, affectionately known as "BO." Bo was a Vietnam Veteran and was in the Army when Agent Orange was released.

I have six siblings and Bo was the only sibling that suffered from these medical issues. Bo had Crohn's Disease and was taking medication that we now know could lead to a rare, but fatal brain disease called CJD.

On February 22, 2018, Bo died from Creutzfeldt-Jakob Diseases known as (CJD). As I write these words, my eyes are filled with tears.

Love and Miss You Big Bo,
Elizabeth Scott aka Liz

Yo, One Shot, I love you so much and I miss you a lot. Thank you for always accepting all of me, good and bad. I learned a lot about life from you. I also learned how to stay strong. When staying strong is my only option. I appreciate all of you and your unconditional love. I will miss your support and long talks because you always supported me in everything I did. You never gave up on me when everybody else turned their back on me. Keep watching over me Pop-Pop, you will always be missed.

Love, Yasir Lewis

Dear Pop-Pop,
Thank you for everything you did for our family and this country. You'll forever be blessed and loved.

Sincerely, Your Grandson Tymir Scott

Hey Pop-Pop,
I miss you so much and thank you for everything you did for me and some! You were and are the best Pop-Pop and father figured I ever had! You were only a phone call away! I appreciate you more than you know! I miss you down here, but I am so happy I could return the favor and take care of you the same way you took care of me! I love you so much.

Love Always, Cupcake Jianae

Thank you, Pop-Pop, for all that you did. Nobody deserved you, but I'm glad we had you. Thanks for serving our country; that's a mess.

Love 2 Shot, Seth

Dad, you are dearly missed and I think of you daily. My heart is heavy from the loss of you and my world will never be the same. I lost my father and a young age and I never wanted to call anyone "Dad" until I met you. You have taught me about life and were always supportive; you were always here for me and Kitten. No matter what the situation was, you would jump in with your advice and a helping hand. I will always love you and consider you as my dad. I love you, Dad, and I know your spirit is still here with me and the family.

Rest-in-Peace

Love, Your Son-in-Law Kevin

Papa Scotty was a great man of God and an amazing family man. I respected him sooo much on how he carried himself; not only as a man, but as a father.

He made the best string beans I have ever eaten and I just wish I could of spent more time with him.

I'm appreciative that when I went to ask him to take his beautiful daughter Marquita to be my wife and he said yes. That meant the world to me to get the chance to ask him while he was still here with us and get his approval. We all Love and Miss you!

Your Son-in Law Furad

TABLE OF CONTENTS

INTRODUCTION

This book is to honor all of the soldiers/Veterans that served in the Vietnam War. The war began on November 1, 1955 and ended on April 30, 1975. However, the U.S. got involved in Vietnam in1954. The United States sent supplies and advisors until 1965.

Most importantly, this book was written to tell the Vietnam Veterans story from their personal experiences. Some of the Veterans we asked said that the experience was too painful to talk or write about. Their concerns were that they would have flashbacks or nightmares as the result of telling their story. It would be like reliving it all over again. Some of them were diagnosed with PTSD (Post Traumatic Stress Disorder). Therefore, we will honor them by listing their names in a section of this book. We will also honor any deceased Veterans, which includes my mother's Jean A. Glover-Scott's late husband Cleveland Scott Jr., known as Big Bo or Scott, and our cousin Hazell Henry McNeely known as Winks. Deborah McNeely will tell the story of her beloved late husband. These two women are their loving wives.

These stories are not easy to read, but they will give you a picture of all they endured to keep our country safe. They are truly remarkable.

It will also educate you regarding Agent Orange and the effects it had on our soldiers. Agent Orange is an herbicide and defoliant chemical. It is widely known for its use by the U.S. military as part of its chemical warfare program during the Vietnam War from 1961 to 1971. Millions of gallons of which had been dumped by U.S. planes on the dense forests of Vietnam.

All of the soldiers were exposed and affected by this chemical. Even their children may have been affected. Some Vets were fortunate to get a diagnosis, but most did not. But as you read through each soldier's story of their experiences, you will agree with my mother and I that many of their health issues were due to Aging Orange, and they did not get the proper health care or respect.

The vision for this book is to show our Vietnam Veterans that we care and appreciate their service. We are sorry that they were not honored and treated as heroes. It breaks our hearts-whenever we see a Vet homeless. After serving our country and suffering the way they did, both the soldier and their immediate families (Wife and children) should never have to ask for anything. They should have been given the royal treatment as if they were celebrities. They shouldn't be concerned about money, housing, health benefits, nor insurance.

We pray that this book will open everyone's eyes regarding the chemical used in the war called Agent Orange and the many health issues it causes for them and children. We want to give our gratitude to Aaron Douglas, the President of Veterans Ministry at Pilgrim Baptist Church, for his diligent service and support of Veterans from every branch and wars. He fights for Veterans' benefits and their rights. His story is included in this book. God Bless the soldiers that made it back home and may the deceased Rest-in Peace.

SECTION ONE

Vietnam Veterans Speaking Out

The Facts: According to Wikipedia

The Vietnam War Chiến Tranh Việt Nam (Vietnamese) is also known as the second Indochina War. However, it was known as the Resistance War Against America or simply the American War in Vietnam. The war was a conflict in various places which includes Vietnam, Laos, and Cambodia from November 1, 1955.

The Paris Peace Accords was signed on January 27, 1973. It included a ceasefire agreement ending the United States involvement in the Vietnam War. The Fall of Saigon occurred on April 30, 1975, when the South Vietnamese government surrendered to the Communists marking the Vietnam War's end.

It was the second of the Indochina Wars. This war was between North Vietnam and South Vietnam. North Vietnam supported the Soviet Union, China, and other communist allies, and South Vietnam was supported by the United States, South Korea, the Philippines, Australia, Thailand, and other anti-communist allies. The war was considered a Cold War that lasted 19 years, five months, four weeks, and one day with direct U.S. involvement ending in 1973.

The Vietnam War was very painful for our nation. There were wounded soldiers, many casualties; simply put, lives were lost.

The Vietnam Conflict Extract Data File of the Defense Casualty

Analysis System (DCAS) Extract Files contains records of 58,220 U.S. military fatal casualties of the Vietnam War. More than 3 million people (including 58,220 Americans) were killed in the Vietnam War, and more than half of the dead were Vietnamese civilians. In addition, to the casualties there were more than 150,000 American soldiers wounded. Therefore, soldiers left to serve in the war, but never returned home. Many soldiers that returned home felt like they were coming to another war because they had to fight for survival.

The true purpose of the Vietnam War was a long, costly, and divisive conflict that pitted the communist government of North Vietnam against South Vietnam and its principal ally, the United States. The conflict was intensified by the ongoing Cold War between the United States and the Soviet Union.

To learn more about the war and its history, go to the website below:

https://www.history.com/topics/vietnam-war/vietnam-war-history

Aaron Douglas

**President of the Pilgrim Baptist Church
Veterans Ministry
MR1 (E6), 8 years – Navy
Naval Support – Danang, Vietnam**

Aaron Douglas

I can only start my story about my time in Vietnam by referring to my time in the United States Navy. After completing boot camp in April 1962, the Navy transferred me to Naval Air Station Atsugi, Japan, for two years. I remember the Cuban Crisis in October 1962 and the death of JFK in November 1963.

I played football for the Atsugi Flyers starting in August 1963. Our team was scheduled to be on "Wide World of Sports," but the game was canceled due to JFK's death.

In April 1964, I was transferred to the USS Kitty Hawk CVA63. The Kitty Hawk planes were flying reconnaissance over North Vietnam. I remember seeing two Kitty Hawk planes with small holes in their wings with a sign saying restricted. It was my first time at sea "The Hawk" stayed at sea for 30 days to support our war effort. When the Kitty Hawk returned to Yokosuka, Japan everyone aboard the ship had to sign a paper stating they would not say anything about their past sea deployment operation.

The Kitty Hawk was home-based out of San Diego, California. Some of the sailors on board receive newspapers from San Diego indicating the Kitty Hawk had two planes shot down off the coast of North Vietnam. We were asked to sign a document, not to talk about our last operation at sea, but in the newspaper.

"The Hawk" was due to transfer back to San Diego. We were waiting for the USS Constellation CVA64 to relive "The Hawk" on station. Then we could steam home to San Diego and then travel to Bremerton, Washington for repairs in the Shipyard. Before going into dry dock, all bombs and missiles were removed from the ship. It was a 24-hour job-total, removing time 60 hours.

I was on the Kitty Hawk for approximately 17 months and volunteered for Vietnam to serve my country. I was a Machinery Repairman 2nd Class E5. (Date of promotion January 1965)

I transferred in August 1965 from USS Kitty Hawk to Camp Pendleton Marine Corp Base. I was there for weapons training and Counter Insurgence School.

I arrived in Vietnam in September 1965 at Naval Support Activity Da Nang, Vietnam. The reporting officer was in an old French building in downtown Da Nang. I was told the floating machine shop would not arrive until December 1965. So, the Navy had to find something for me to do. Da Nang had a large harbor, and the supplies came in by ships to support the war effort. There were no peers deep enough, so the ships anchored out.

Supplies were offloaded to small Navy vessels call Mike 6, Mike 8, and LCU. The Navy finally found a job for me delivering mail to the sailors on the small boats. I delivered mail to over 100 sailors. You did not need a stamp; only had to write "free" in the upper right corner.

I'm a maintenance repair person and did not have a repair shop to do any work. I spent a lot of time in downtown, Da Nang near the headquarters for Naval Support Activity.

There was a large Military PX about 5 miles from downtown Da Nang. I enjoy communicating with local people. They were friendly and had many craft skills.

When I first arrived in Da Nang, I ate and slept on a Navy ship called Okanogan (APA 220) anchored in the harbor. As part of North Vietnam propaganda, we would hear music played on the radio. One night, Hanoi Hannah stated, "Okanogan, this is your last night; your ship tomorrow morning will be sunk in Da Nang Harbor." Well, the next day, I was on my job. Remember, I'm still delivering mail and picked it up 2 to 3 times a day from 20 small boats that the Navy had in the harbor receiving supplies.

In December 1965, two APL (floating Barracks) were transported to Da Nang as living quarters.

In early 1966, I was relieved of my duties as a mailman and transferred to the Philippines to finish outfitting a floating machine shop.

I spent eight weeks in the Philippines before the floating machine shop was transferred to Da Nang, around late March 1966. Travel time from the Philippines to Da Nang was 3 ½ days being towed by an ocean tug.

The floating Repair Shop had a machine shop, welding shop, and an electric shop on the lower level. The Topside was living quarters and a mess hall. We also had two washers/dryers and bathing showers.

Also, both levels on the floating machine shop were air-conditioned.

Da Nang has many white sandy beaches. I can remember using our motorboat to view and drink beer on the beach. When we arrived, the Marines came out of the bush and asked us, "Why are you guys here today? Intelligence tells us the VC is coming through here tonight." Our beach party was over and we motored back to the machine shop.

As the sun was setting, we could see the flares lighting up the sky along the beaches where we had stopped to drink beer. Before the night was over, the flares were above the machine shop. Remember, we're on a floating machine shop, we're anchored out, and we do not have the power to get underway. I was scared; I didn't know what to do, so I went to Topside and went to sleep. I woke up the next day and everything was back to normal.

I enjoyed my tour in Vietnam. I valued the friendships I made along the way. I volunteered to go to Vietnam and reenlisted for four years in January 1966. During my tour in Vietnam, I made two RR trips; Kaohsiung City, Taiwan, and Tokyo, Japan. I transferred from Da Nang to the USS Tidewater AD 31 in late August 1966. I was promoted to E6 (Machinery Repairman 1st Class) in February 1967.

The Tidewater traveled to Naples, Italy, in March 1967. On a day off, I traveled to the Ancient Roman City of Pompeii. In late March, I transferred back to the USA because the ship moved from Naples to Gibraltar because of Israel's problems.

I arrived in Washington, DC, in April 1967 and attended a career counseling school. I served as Career Counselor Naval District Washington DC until January 27, 1970. My military career came to an end.

God Bless America; I will always love my country. I served eight years in the US Navy for my country.

"You can take the man out of the Navy, but you cannot take the Navy out of the man."

With the Love of Family, Aaron Lamar Douglas

Summary

I was married when I returned from Vietnam and living in Bremerton, Washington, a military city.

I do not have any problems with Agent Orange, but my M-spike, also called monoclonal immunoglobulin in my blood work, is above normal. Therefore, I have it checked twice a year. I have been denied benefits two times. However, I received a letter from the VA to re-submit my claim in October 2019.

Rocky L. Hammond Sr.

Rocky L. Hammond Sr.

I was drafted into the Army as a Construction Engineer. My tour of duty in Vietnam was from January 1969 to February 1970. When I received my orders to go to Vietnam, **I FELT LIKE** I was going to death row. After telling my family, my oldest brother said, "I guess I won't see you anymore."

There was daily fighting in Vietnam, seeing my fellow soldiers killed, young Vietnamese (who looked like children) were fighting and being killed. I then realized why my commanders told us not to make friends because I may not see some of my fellow soldiers anymore. I felt that every day was my last day to live.

I was in Vietnam for three months when my position changed from a Construction Engineer to a Combat Engineer. And with one week of training, my new duties were to look for hidden/buried explosives. In addition to these duties, I was still in the line of fire and being shot at. While there, you always had to be in survival mode.

At night, they would drop mortars (rockets) at us. We had to fall out on the firing line and we had to return fire. I was shooting a 50-caliber machine gun. At daybreak, we had to find the Vietcong bodies and bury them. We dressed in white suits and had to pick up the dead bodies with our hands covered with long gloves. The dead bodies were thrown into a front-end loader. The bulldozer would dig a big hole and dozens of bodies were dump in that hole. We put lime over the bodies and the bulldozer would cover up the hole and roll over the man-made grave to pack the ground. I would throw up because the ground looked like jelly and my eyes would fill up with tears. While being in Vietnam, you would think all the soldiers would get along mainly for survivorship. However, there was a high degree of racial tension.

My sergeant put me in charge to set up an ambush control. A White soldier who had rank over me pulled his rank and told me that I was setting up the ambush control wrong and told me to set it up his way. His way was the wrong way (we were facing each other). Fortunately, that night, there was no fighting because we would have been shooting at each other if it had been.

This same White soldier and a Black soldier started fighting in the bunkers. I broke up the fight by grabbing the Black soldier and another White soldier grabbed the other soldier. When we thought the fight was over, the White soldier was still being held. When I let the Black soldier go, he ran out of the bunkers after hitting the White soldier down. When I saw this White soldier pick up his M16 and started shooting at me, I started running and the bullets went into the sandbags. While shooting, he was yelling, "All you N…. are in this S---- together!" If I had been two seconds slower, he would have hit me in the back. He still had his M16 in his hands when everyone came out of their bunkers. The sergeants came out and asked what happened? After explaining the situation, the White soldier got a slap on his wrist by putting him in another barrage which housed all White soldiers. My captain told me that I could have him court-martialed. He said I would have had to stay in Vietnam for additional six months until the court-martial was over. My Vietnam tour would have been over in two months; therefore, I did not have him court-martialed because I did not want to extend my stay in Vietnam.

About a month later, our soldiers had to put down asphalt and a group of us had to do road security to protect them while working. This same White soldier was on the bulldozer pushing brush. As road security, our job was also to tell the soldiers to keep up with the group (we had to be in columns). One of the other soldiers told me to tell this White soldier to catch up. I refused to tell him because he was the same one who pulled rank on me and shot at me with his M16.

A half-hour later, the Vietcong started dropping mortars. When the shooting started, the same White soldier jumped off his bulldozer. Then he started running into the woods which was the opposite way from us running with his M16 in his hand. When the shooting stopped, we realized he was missing. We looked for him and found him tied up to a rubber tree with wire around his hands, legs, and throat. His body was completely shot up with bullets (execution-style). We had to take his body down because we never leave American bodies.

How I Felt Being Back Home

When I returned to the states, I thought I would have received a warm welcome from friends and family. There was little to no compassion from people in the U.S. I felt lost and could not understand why I was called a child killer, spit at, and robbed because people probably knew that arriving back in the states, we had "mustard pay" and all our vacation pay. Back then, no one would hire Vietnam Vets.

Two Major Things that Bothers Me

There are so many things that bother me. However, the two major things are: First, there were only three 50 caliber machine guns and I had one of them. We couldn't see people; we only saw red traces. A very young boy was in my line of fire, and I may have killed him; his entire right shoulder was gone (he may have bled to death). The other two soldiers both were claiming that they shot him. I refused to take claim that it was my machine gun that killed him. The second, was the racial tension amongst the Blacks and Whites. They used to fly rebel flags over their bunkers. A Black soldier flew a red, green, and black flag; the captain told the Black soldier to take his flag down because that is an African flag and the rebel flag is an American flag.

The Conclusion

I did not know anything about Post Traumatic Stress Disorder (PTSD); however, after returning home, I started doing things that I never did before. I was still in survival mode and thinking bombs were being thrown. I would hear cars backfire and I would drop to the ground trying to take cover. My wife and I were sleeping and I found myself choking my wife, thinking she was the enemy.

It took me eight years to become a 100% disabled Vet. This

disability has many financial benefits; however, it does not compensate for exposing me to Agent Orange, to the chemical (Round-Up) which is a contributing factor for me getting cancer. The traumatic stress, thinking that I may have killed children. I had to see a therapist because I cannot see anyone buried due to the flashbacks of seeing how bodies on top of bodies of the Vietcong's thrown into man-made graves.

To my knowledge, I do not believe nothing is documented on rather being exposed to this toxic chemical and having PTSD could have negative birth defects (mental or physical) to my children.

I was diagnosed with stage 4 cancer and I thank God every day that I am now cancer-free.

Ira Kirch

Ira Kirch

In June 1968, I graduated from the University of Delaware, then two weeks later, I went into the Army. In March 1969, I went to Vietnam; I was assigned to II Field's Forces, an artillery division that operated in three corps in Saigon and the surrounding province. I was assigned to a 105MM battery at the Special Forces camp at KATUM on the Cambodia borderline. Our battery was split between KATUM and another Special Forces camp. We were three guns between 30 to 40 men. There were the Special Forces people about 10 and 200 or so Cambodian mercenaries. I was there for six months until our battery was withdrawn. I spent the next six months with a 159 battery; we moved several times, but always on the Cambodia border.

In March 1970, I came home and I felt our mission was correct to stop the communist. Most of the people did not want to have anything to do with the communists. Many fled from Vietnam when the communists took over. MacArthur was right, don't fight a land war on Asia. President Johnson should have dropped the "A" bomb on Havoc. No war could have saved a million lives.

In Vietnam, I learned not to be sorry about what I have no control over. If your number was up, it was up.

When I came home, I was discharged and then began civilian life. Delaware was unrecognized in life, but a bonus of $200.00 was given to Vietnam Veterans which was not a lot back then, but a nice thank you. I was lucky that I was not injured or that I suffered any illness.

John Langjahr

John Langjahr

I t started in early '68, I received a notice to report to the Beury Building located in Broad and Erie vicinity in Philadelphia, PA, for a physical exam to be rated for the draft. After the physical exam, I was informed that I was rated 1-A, which meant I was eligible for the draft. Then there was the draft induction formality.

The man said, "All those willing to be inducted into the draft, take one step forward." Of course, I did, as well as everyone else.

In June, I received a card from the LBJ, informing me that I would be drafted. At that point in time, I was employed at Connelly Containers in Bala Cynwyd and living in Nicetown. I received a ride from a co-worker to Greene and Penn Street; from there, I would run to the 4500 block of Gratz Street where I lived. I would run to get into condition.

I left for boot camp on June 17, 1968. My older sister Janet drove me to 30th Street and I got the train for Fayetteville, NC Fort Bragg. There was a military-type bus waiting to take us to the base. We were driven to get supplies that were issued in duffel bags. Then we were instructed to take our civilian clothes off and we were issued fatigue uniforms. The Supply Sergeant issued the Khaki uniforms, but they didn't have any uniforms in my size, which was a 38. Therefore, I was issued a size 36.

Then I was told, "When it's all over son, they'll fit."

After that, a Drill Sergeant stood in the doorway and yelled,

"Everybody outside!" So we went out and it was dark (pitch-black).

The sergeant said, "When I say 'Formation' I want four lines of you people lined up straight and even. You will stand at 'Attention' until given the command 'At Ease.'"

It was a dark and warm-humid night. We were instructed to place our duffel bags on one shoulder and follow the Drill Sergeant running to the Barracks. At the Barracks, we were assigned racks, which were beds.

Immediately, the sergeant said, "While you people are here, you will learn how hard housekeeping is. The work your mother's do for you at home." Then he demonstrated exactly how he wanted the beds made with hospital corners.

Getting back to basic training, it was eight weeks of Hell, but I was proud to have made it. The whole time I was in basic training, my feet hurt really bad. I had callouses on the balls of my feet. It felt like nails were being driven into my feet. Therefore, I wrote home and asked my mom if she would mail me a pair of Dr. Scholl's Foot Pads shoe inserts. Fortunately, my mom sent the shoe inserts and the pain did subside. I didn't go on a sick call because the Drill Sergeant would think we were slacking.

There was one area I hated; it was called the Mulch Pit. The Mulch Pit was an area about 25ft by 25ft. A person would crawl on their hands and knees until the Drill Sergeant was satisfied. Another area was the Company Area with five Barracks; a platoon was assigned to each Barracks. The street around the Barracks was made up of the stones that are placed between train tracks. On one occasion, the Drill Sergeant was angry about something and he ordered the platoon to low crawl with elbows and knees around the Barracks. The elbows and knees of my wore out with traces of blood.

On one hot day, we walked to a Rifle Range. We were told it was miles and the roads were all sand like on a beach.

Someone yelled out, "Don't they have roads down here!"

The sergeant replied, "They didn't have roads at Normandy in World War II."

Then he said, "When you people go overseas, you don't know what it will be like. So, we want you ready."

While walking down the sand trail, we encountered a sign that said, *"It is Better to Sweat in Peace Time than Bleed in War."*

After we all qualified at the Rifle Range, we marched back to the company area. The sergeant told me and three others to walk in front of the platoon. We were the biggest guys in the platoon.

The sergeant said, "If any of these M*** F*** fall out, walk over them."

I want to tell you, I'm proud to say I made it as well as the other three. The assembly area was a blacktop parking lot. I could see heat waves coming up from the ground.

When the formation was over, the sergeant yelled, "Dismissed!"

Everyone ran to the Barracks to get a cold drink of water from the water fountain. When I got there, it was a long line, so I went to the shower area. I took off my uniform, boots, and socks and went into a nice cool shower. At that point in time, basic training was almost over. I had just one more week.

The next phase was the night obstacle course; we would start out climbing up a ladder. At the top of the ladder, there was a machine gun firing overhead; it was about 50 yards away. We were instructed to low crawl, keep down, and stay down. After that, it was downhill.

Also, during basic training, it was found out the sergeant was hungover. I heard he was busted for that and I never saw him again. Shortly afterward, we were finished basic training. I was sent to Ft. Lewis, VA, where I attended school for special purchase repair parts; the course was four weeks.

The Mess Hall at Ft. Lewis was very nice. The tables had tablecloths and there was a sign on the wall that read: *"Welcome Home."* They even had other soldiers acting like waiters.

We were asked, "How would you like your steak?" This was a very nice memory.

After that, I attended another class for stock control and accounting. Also, a four-week course. Then I was on a four-week leave and on December 31, 1968, I boarded a plane to Ft. Lewis, Washington. Actually, the flight was to Seattle, Washington. I spent New Years' evening on a jet plane. I was at Ft. Lewis for several days, then one morning I boarded a flight to Tokyo with a 4-hour layover. I boarded a plane headed to Naha, Okinawa from Tokyo, and there was another layover and transfer to another plane. The destination was Cam Ranh Bay Vietnam.

After spending several days, I traveled approximately 200 miles to Qui Nhon. During the flight, we encountered what we thought was turbulence. But after we landed, we found out it was not turbulence but anti-aircraft fire. I thought to myself, *"I only been here a couple of hours and being shot already."*

In addition, I was assigned to an outside supply area. During the dry season (the summer) was all dust and the temperature could reach 100 degrees. And during the rainy season (a monsoon), it was nothing but mud. After a while, I would walk through the mud without concern over getting muddled.

One morning after a rainstorm, a rocket-propelled and grenade landed in the mud and did not explode. It wasn't far from my bunk area.

Every company on the compound had to provide a perimeter guard. We also provided guard duty at the fuel depot. The mindset we got fuel there, we guarded there. Fortunately, nothing happened on the two occasions I had guard duty there. While on the perimeter guarding a tower, I spotted a man walking outside the fence along-side a water buffalo. His position was approximately 50 yards to my left.

I radioed the activity to the C-Q (Command Quarters) and was told to, "Do not shoot the man or the animal. Shoot the machine gun over his head."

Therefore as instructed, I didn't shoot the old man nor the animal. Because if I shot and killed them, it would have been considered an illegal kill.

After the old man left the area, the Security Platoon arrived with a truck. On the back of the truck was an M-50 machine gun mounted on a turret; man was that thing loud. They shot up the hillside, thinking it may have been a diversion tactic.

While in Qui Nhon, I believe I had a paranormal experience. While on tower guard, one night in a remote dark area, I was tired and sleepy. I used water from my canteen to stay awake by splashing it on my face.

All of a sudden, I heard a voice call, "Jack, wake up!"

I thought the voice was coming from a cave or an echo room. It scared the Hell out of me. However, nothing happened that night. It is ironic, 58,000 Americans lost their lives over there and Saigon fell to the communist.

Now it's time for graduation and family came to see us graduate. My parents and my older sister came down. It was a time I'll never forget. I'm proud to say I went through the experience, but **NEVER AGAIN!**

Joel McCormick

Joel McCormick

The Vietnam Era, through the eyes of Joel McCormick. The war in Vietnam was going on when I graduated high school in 1968. Men across the country were given Selective Service numbers and placed in specific classification categories. Men were being drafted and placed in the military. Many were inducted into the United States Army. Some volunteered to serve in other branches of the military. I like others, volunteered and entered the United States Air Force on the 3rd day of August 1970.

My unique experience began at my 1st assignment while being stationed at Little Rock Air Force Base, Arkansas. One day, I went to volunteer for another assignment in Vietnam. Following the brief assignment at Little Rock, my preparation began for my next assignment in South East Asia. My next assignment was Da Nang Air Base Vietnam.

During the summer months preceding late November 1971, knowing I would be serving my country in Vietnam, the words **Excitement** and **Anticipation** best describes my feelings. Having attained the age of 22 a few months earlier, there was also a sense of Patriotism. After all, I enlisted and volunteered for Nam.

On the TV, newspapers and radio were information about the war and its casualties. However, on the other hand, such leaders Martin Luther King Jr., Rap Brown, Huey P. Newton, Stokely Carmichael, and others were much opposed to the war. Being a young man and like many young African Americans, there was a feeling of being **Untouchable, Fearless,** and not worried about **Dying.** Yet, my sanity also let me know there was a possibility that I might be injured or become one of the fallen. Da Nang Air

Base had a nickname Rocket City (Charlie another name for the Viet Cong) launched mortars, resulting in casualties and injuries.

Upon arriving at Da Nang Air Base, late November 1971, I spoke to a fellow airman I knew from technical school while stationed in Illinois.

"Hey Mac," (individuals in Armed Forces sometimes have nick names like others in our society like sports, etc., "we are going to be stationed in Thailand." Mine was Mac.

By Divine Providence, I spent one week in Vietnam and a few days in Saigon awaiting transportation to Thailand, where I would spend the next 12 months.

The Vietnamese that I saw in Vietnam was short in stature and many lived poorly. One thing I noticed, one did not know most of the time friend or foe; people went about their daily activities and knew you were American, so you always wanted to be aware of your surroundings.

In Thailand daily living was somewhat different. We were not at war with Thai people. Still, always be vigilant about your surroundings. The entire year's duty hours were day shift consisting of 12-hour shifts. My daily routine did not change much due to my working 12-hour shifts. Yes, we supported the Vietnam War with missions that flew out of Thailand. The days not working my routine changed somewhat. All the days of the week were all the same to me. It didn't matter which day one had off from work.

Military personnel boosted the economy in Vietnam, Thailand, and South East Asia by purchasing goods, such as clothing, shoes, suits etc. Thai women would share food with other women in their village so that no one went without. I have experienced **unity** among African Americans among Veterans in Thailand. I have experienced solidarity among African

Americans and used it myself on numerous occasions while being stationed in Thailand.

DAP (Dignity and Pride) It started as a symbol of unity and sign to Black soldiers during the Vietnam war that they had each other's back. Giving dap typically involves handshaking (often by hoking thumbs), pound hugging, fist pounding, or chest - or fist bumping. The term originated among Black soldiers during the Vietnam War, as part of the Black Power Movement, and the term is attested around 1969. Giving dap - Wikipedia

Truth be told, I was glad and happy to be on American soil. Having arrived in Seattle, Washington no place like home. When I returned to New Jersey, there was no fanfare, no party, no parade, or celebrations. In fact, I didn't really expect special recognition or treatment. My parents, brothers, and relatives were glad and happy to see me home again. Veterans were afforded some preference toward some employers in the workplace. Individuals that knew me prior to enlisting in the military were glad to see and know that I was home.

In conclusion, Veterans that were departing Thailand would on their last day of work somehow were splashed with water symbolizing their tour was ended.

My question is:

How are we receiving Veterans today that are returning from war that have been in theater compared to then and now?

The Late Hazell Henry McNeely
Aka Winks

Received the "Purple Heart for Bravery"

The Late Hazell Henry McNeely aka Winks

My name is Deborah McNeely, the widow of The Late Hazell Henry McNeely, better known as Winks to his family and friends. I am honored to share Winks experience in Vietnam.

In 1968 he entered the United States Army and was sent to Vietnam to fight in the war. He told us the story about his first gunfight, either the Vietnamese.

Everyone was shooting and he froze and couldn't shoot his gun until the Sergeant put a gun to his head and said, "You shoot that gun now Boy or I'm gonna shoot you!" He was so afraid that he wet his pants, but he shot the gun.

After several gunfights and witnessing several of his friends being killed, he was wounded and sent to Japan for R and R. Winks was honorably discharged with a Purple Heart for his bravery.

He felt betrayed by the government when he got home and often said that he would never fight for them again.

After several years of health problems, in 1988, he had his first heart attack but didn't address his medical problems with the VA (Veterans Administration) until 1996. He was diagnosed with Agent Orange. Every summer, he suffered from Jungle rock where his hands would get blisters.

In 2005, I (his wife) began to write letters to the VA asking for compensation for his heart disease, Agent Orange, back, and leg pain. In 2007, he was awarded 100% disability.

Through the years, Winks suffered from 15 heart attacks, high blood pressure, diabetes, coronary heart disease, and PTSD. He was put on hospice on February 12, 2014. He passed away August 5, 2014, from heart complications.

Lovingly Submitted,

His Beloved Wife, Deborah McNeely

The Late Cleveland Scott Jr.

Aka Big Bo

SP4-E4

The Late Cleveland Scott Jr. aka Big Bo

My name is Jean A. Glover-Scott; I am the widow of the Late Cleveland Scott Jr. He served in the Army, ranked as an SP4-E4. My husband and I talked a lot about his experience in Vietnam. Therefore, I will try to tell his story on his behalf.

"When I first got over to Vietnam, I didn't know what to expect," Scott said, "because the conditions were bad." You see, Scott didn't know if he was going ever to make it back home.

He was stationed in Cam Ranh Bay. Cam Ranh Bay is a deep-water bay in Vietnam in Khánh Hòa Province. It is located at an inlet of the South China Sea situated on the southeastern coast of Vietnam, between Phan Rang and Nha Trang, approximately 290 kilometers northeast of Ho Chi Minh City.

It was a blessing to be stationed there because it was safer than any other place in Vietnam. However, Scott shared in detail that the U.S. soldiers were informed that the Vietcong Snipers were coming across the water trying to ambush them. Therefore, he and the other soldiers had to shoot their guns quickly. It was dark and they couldn't see anything. Therefore, they didn't know if they killed the Vietcong Snipers. However, when morning came, Scott said dead bodies were floating in the water.

So I asked him, "Do you think that you killed any of them?"

He replied, "I don't know; I just shot my gun; it was too dark."

Fortunately, that was the only time they had to fight for their lives. Scott's other major concern was that Agent Orange was sprayed everywhere and that he was consuming it.

Scott told me that he drank, played cards, listen to music, and joked with fellow soldiers to pass the time away. He was stationed there for two years from September 8, 1966, until September 6, 1968, and then returned home.

When he returned home, he was disappointed because he felt that his service was unappreciated. He felt that he and the other fellow soldiers did not receive a warm welcome back home or any respect at all. They even were called "Baby Killers" and spit on to name a few.

Two years later, we became pregnant. My daughter Larenda was born in 1970 and started having multiple health issues in 1981 at the young age of 11, which continues today.

Our next child was conceived about a year later. Our daughter Sharnika was born in 1971 and she also has health issues. Scott felt that his children were also affected by Agent Orange because it was in his system.

In 2011, his major health issues started. Scott was diagnosed with a heart condition and digestive system issues. Scott believed it was due to Agent Orange. Agent Orange is an herbicide and defoliant chemical, one of the "tactical use" Rainbow Herbicides. It is widely known for its use by the U.S. military as part of its chemical warfare program, Operation Ranch Hand, during the Vietnam War from 1961 to 1971. Due to the chemical, Agent Orange was sprayed everywhere and he felt that was the major factor why he started getting ill. He even applied for Veterans benefits but was denied.

Later, he was diagnosed with Crohn's Disease; his diagnosis date is unknown. Scott managed his Crohn's Disease fairly well. However, in December 2017, he became suddenly ill. He called our daughter Kitten and said, "Kitten, my hand is shaking; I'm going to the hospital."

She replied, "Do you want me to take to the hospital, Dad?"

"No, by the time you get your butt here, I'll be at the hospital."

Kitten said, "Okay, I'll meet you there."

They admitted him for a short stay, approximately a week, and sent him home. He was upset because he still didn't feel well and felt that he did not get the right diagnoses. He became worse, he was shaking more, falling up the steps, losing his balance, and didn't have any energy; he was really fatigued.

Christmas Eve, my neighbor took him back to the hospital. He was admitted and had various testing. The neurologist diagnosed him with "Mad Cow Disease," And because only cattle get Mad Cow disease, the family, especially his children, did not accept the diagnosis. Therefore, they had him transported to Philadelphia, PA, for a second opinion.

Unfortunately, my husband started deteriorating daily and they diagnosed him with Creutzfeldt-Jakob Disease known as , which is extremely rare. It is the human form of Mad Cow Disease. is a degenerative brain disorder that leads to dementia and death. He was hospitalized for about two months and he suffered. Eventually, he stops walking, talking, and eating. He was in extreme pain. When the hospital felt nothing else they could do for him, they released him to go home on hospice.

Sadly, he departed this life at home with family and me by his side on February 21, 2018, approximately at 11:53 pm, but officially pronounced by hospice on February 22, 2018.

We did apply for Veterans benefits but again was denied. They claim that there was no evidence that the Creutzfeldt-Jakob Disease was manifested to a compensable within one year of the Veterans discharge from service for presumptive consideration. Based on these findings, entitlement to service connection cause for the Veterans death is denied since evidence fails to show that it was related to his military service.

My family and I feel that the heart disease, Crohn's, and CJD are related to Agent Orange the chemical that was sprayed in Vietnam manifested later in his life.

I want to thank my husband for his service in the military and may he Rest-in-Peace. He was laid to rest in the Veterans Cemetery.

Lovingly Submitted from his Beloved Wife,

Jean A. Glover-Scott

Phillip Ward

U.S. Army Artillery 333rd Arty, 6th Arty Op SP4 (T)

Honorable Discharge

Radio Operator 12/14/67 - 02/06/69

National Defense Service Medal. Expert Rifle.

Vietnam Service Medal w/2 Bronze stars.

Republic of Vietnam Campaign Medal w/Device

Phillip Ward's Memorabilia

Phillip Ward

My daddy suffers every single day from Agent Orange. Upon returning home from his tour, my mom got pregnant. My brother's birthday is tomorrow. He would have been 50. He would have been handsome, kind, and generous. He would have a family of his own. That was taken from my brother. My brother was taken from us. Thank you, AGENT ORANGE!

My dad was sprayed & covered in this chemical...

"they said it was safe."

"they said no side effects."

"they said Agent Orange effects are not debilitating."

Ask my dad Phillip Ward Sr., Vietnam Vet from 1967 to 1968. Radio Operator, Advanced Jungle Training, Minor League Softball, Committee Man; Healthy...THEN.

Now, in pain every day. Kidney, liver, and severe abdominal issues, headaches, a diabetic, and has night terrors. He is not as strong but continues on. My dad doesn't even get to enjoy the July 4th fireworks.

My dad, my family, was covered in a chemical the U.S.A. tried to deny its deadly effects. We were not in Vietnam with my dad, but once he came home, we unwittingly joined him in his terror; Vietnam, my family, is affected by this chemical, the USA swore was safe. My brother...he survived, almost 16 years requiring 24 hr. non-stop nursing care. He was so small that he slept in a crib for infants, sat in a highchair, and couldn't feed himself; my family was heartbroken. My brother Phillip Ward Jr. died painfully the day after Valentines' Day more than 30 years ago. Vietnam war has long been over. But its effects continue.

Thank you to all the soldiers for your courage, your service, and your sacrifice.

ALL MY LOVE, YOU ARE MY HERO!

Lovingly Submitted,

Your daughter Angie Ward

Harold Richard Williams

Harold Richard Williams

Welcome Home! Vietnam/Post Vietnam Memories

I arrived in The Republic of South Vietnam in March of 1969. I was only 19-years-old and I had just left a carefree life, where I thought war was exactly like what I had seen in the movies or on television. My first memories of Vietnam were how hot it was and how the horrible stench filled my nose once debarking the plane. It was 7 pm and the thermometer read 97 degrees. Little did I know that some of the smell was from the 55-gallon half drums under the latrines, containing human waste that had to be removed, and burned each evening. The rest of the smell was just Vietnam at that time.

I served with the Green Berets (5th Special Forces Group), Army Intelligence, as an Order of Battle Analyst. That was my title, but not necessarily my actual job. Like most Vietnam Vets, we ended up doing more jobs than our MOS called for. My other jobs consisted of working on the Mobile Strike Force, 82mm Mortar Crew, developing post-combat film in the darkroom & showing movies in the chow hall in the evenings when time allowed. I saw my share of action and unfortunately, more than my share of death.

Although I rarely distinguished between races, I did notice for the first time in my life how close the Brothers were. No matter which unit or what part of the war zone they were stationed. From Corps to the Mekong Delta, I often met fellow Black Soldiers that I had never seen before. It felt as though we were best friends and had known one another for a lifetime. But, the other side of the race issue was the way the military differentiated between the Black & White Soldiers. I realize now, more so than I did then, that my fellow White Soldiers weren't at fault. But, their promotions in rank came at a rate three times faster than that of the Black Soldiers.

Returning Home

Upon returning home and being honorably discharged from the Army. I rarely discussed with my family or friends anything having to do with my time in the war zone. Why? When I returned from Vietnam, this country was going through tumultuous social and political upheavals. The war was a very unpopular war and from the way we Vietnam Vets were greeted with disdain, I felt it was wise for me to not mention my involvement to anyone. In my mind, we were just young soldiers, stripped of our youth, sent off to a foreign land to fight in a war we did not ask for and were just doing our jobs. But, far too many viewed us as terrorists and baby killers. At that time, this caused me to have a lot of self-doubt and shame concerning my role in the Vietnam Conflict. (It had not been declared a war yet)

Forty years had passed before I found myself confronted by Vietnam again. This was because I found out that I had cancer due to Agent Orange that was used in the war zone by our own government. Much to my chagrin, I also was diagnosed with PTSD (Post Traumatic Stress Disorder). I thought this couldn't possibly be right until I thought back on how I had failed at my first marriage, estranged myself from my children, destroyed future relationships with women, friends, and co-workers. I was often in a heightened state of anger. Fortunately, after almost sabotaging my second marriage, I finally got help from the Veterans Affairs Department. I took classes at the Philadelphia Vet Center and I stayed in their program for over two years. I took three different phases of their recovery program.

Upon completion, I was asked to take part in a new program that was being implemented. The reason I was asked was because they thought that I was so messed up when I first started. Therefore, who was more qualified to reach other PTSD sufferers than me! They asked me to be an Assistant Teacher of PTSD to veterans who had returned home from Vietnam, Iraq, and Afghanistan. I taught PTSD for four years until I moved from the Philadelphia area.

Agent Orange

I've been affected in numerous ways from Agent Orange. As mentioned above, I had Prostate Cancer, as well as suffering from Peripheral Neuropathy. I've been blessed to have my cancer removed and am currently in remission. However, there is no cure for the pain of Neuropathy nor the mental anguish of PTSD. These are things that, through the years, I've learned to live with. The one thing that I question is how Agent Orange may have also affected my two children. One contracted cancer when she was 11-years-old and the other has had to deal with a compromised immune system most of her adult life.

All in all, I would have to say the Vietnam War was a blessing, as well as a curse for me. It forced me to grow into a man very quickly, yet, I've had to pay with how I suffered physically and mentally. I will also say this, and I mean it from the bottom of my heart: "If I could do a year in Vietnam, there's nothing, other than God, that I fear out here!"

Lastly, I'd like to say how much I appreciate the positive recognition that we Vietnam Veterans are finally receiving. Nothing feels better than to have someone I may know, or perfect strangers, reach out to shake my hand and thank me for my service or to hear them say, "Welcome Home!"

Short Memories by Harold Richard Williams

SECTION TWO

Thank You for Your Service

I n this section, we will share a few Vietnam Veterans affected in some way by their experience in Vietnam. Some have PTSD or do not want to relive their traumatic journey. Therefore, they cannot share their story, but we still wanted to honor them by thanking them for their service, sacrifice, and letting them know they are appreciated. Most importantly, our prayers are with them. We have also mentioned our brothers in Christ from Pilgrim Baptist Church.

Robert H. Carr

Vietnam Veteran

William M. Cottingham aka Cotton

Served from 1967 to 1968

Stationed in Fort Worth, Texas

"Special Forces" Ammunition and Explosives

Cotton suffers from PTSD

Jerry Flowers Sr.

Sp 5, 2 years – Army
27th Engineer Bn. – Phu Bai Vietnam

Sgt. Earnest Hill

3 years – Army,
1st Calvary – Vietnam

1st Sgt. EB Charles Porter

23 years – Army
Helicopter Mech HU1B – Vietnam

Thank you for your Service

SECTION THREE

About Agent Orange

Agent Orange is an herbicide and defoliant chemical, one of the "tactical use" Rainbow Herbicides. It is widely known for its use by the U.S. military as part of its chemical warfare program, Operation Ranch Hand, during the Vietnam War from 1961 to 1971. It is a mixture of equal parts of two herbicides, 2,4,5-T, and 2,4-D. In addition to its damaging environmental effects, traces of dioxin (mainly TCDD, the most toxic of its type) found in the mixture have caused many exposed individuals' major health problems.

Up to four million people in Vietnam were exposed to the defoliant. The government of Vietnam says as many as three million people have suffered illness because of Agent Orange, and the Red Cross of Vietnam estimates that up to one million people are disabled or have health problems as a result of Agent Orange contamination. The United States government has described these figures as unreliable while documenting higher leukemia cases, Hodgkin's lymphoma, and various kinds of cancer in exposed US military veterans. An epidemiological study done by the Centers for Disease Control and Prevention showed an increase in the rate of birth defects in military personnel children due to Agent Orange. Agent Orange has also caused enormous environmental damage in Vietnam. Over 3,100,000 hectares (31,000 km or 11,969 mi) of forest were defoliated. Defoliants eroded tree cover and seedling forest stock, making reforestation difficult in numerous areas. Animal species diversity sharply reduced in contrast with unsprayed areas.

The use of Agent Orange in Vietnam resulted in numerous legal actions. The United Nations ratified United Nations General Assembly Resolution 31/72 and the Environmental Modification Convention. Lawsuits filed on behalf of both U.S. and Vietnamese veterans sought compensation for damages.

The British Armed Forces first used Agent Orange in Malaya during the Malayan Emergency. The U.S. military in Laos and Cambodia during the Vietnam War because the Viet Cong forests near the Vietnam border were used. The herbicide was also used in Brazil to clear out sections of land for agriculture.

Agent Orange Registry Health Exam for Veterans

The VA's Agent Orange Registry Health Exam alerts Veterans to possible long-term health problems that may be related to Agent Orange exposure during their military service. The registry data helps VA understand and respond to these health problems more effectively. Contact your local **VA Environmental Health Coordinator** about getting an Agent Orange Registry health exam.

Resource

https://www.publichealth.va.gov/exposures/agentorange/benefits/reg istry-exam.asp

SECTION FOUR

The Memorial Wall

We give our heartfelt thanks to all you that have served in Vietnam and was Casualty of War. You will never be forgotten. Below is the number of causalities reported in alphabetical.

Vietnam casualties the letter represents the last name of the soldiers that were killed by serving their country in Vietnam:

A 1784	G 3041	M 5546	SS 5797	Y 308
B 5510	H 4468	N 993	T 2133	Z 218
C 4372	I 218	On 826	U 154	
D 2795	J 1848	P 2285	V 771	
E 1082	K 2043	Q 117	W 3757	
F 1984	L 2600	R 3023	X 1	

If you would like to view the soldiers that have lost their precious lives serving our country. Please go to the website to view their names at http://virtualwall.org/da/0a.htm. You can see the entire list of Vietnam War Casualties by name in alphabetical order on the Memorial Wall.

Our research learned that an estimated 47,434 American soldiers were killed in battle during the Vietnam War, which spanned from 1964 to 1975. An additional 10,786 died in the theater of war but out of battle, making a total of 58,220 deaths.

SECTION FIVE

Facts About Veterans Day

As an American, you know that Veterans Day is a well-known holiday and is celebrated by most. However, there are a few misconceptions about it.

For instance, how is Veterans Day spelled, or whom exactly are we celebrating? Well, this section will help clear up five facts that you should know.

1. Veterans Day DOES NOT have an apostrophe. Some spell it Veteran's Day or Veterans' Day in which both are incorrect. It is simply Veterans Day. The reason being the holiday is not a day that honors only one veteran or multiple veterans. It honors ALL veterans. Therefore no apostrophe is needed and using one incorrect.

2. Memorial Day vs. Veterans Day; Memorial Day is a time to reflect and remember those who gave their lives for our country all branches (Army, Navy, Airforce or Marines, and all wars; not just Vietnam). It's is used to observe those who in battle or from wounds they suffered in battle. Veterans Days honors all of those who have served in the country in war or peace, whether they are deceased or living. This day is set aside to thank the living veteran for their service and sacrifices. I feel both should be celebrated daily, meaning we should daily thank all men and women for their service and never forget any of them. Although this book is

tailored towards Vietnam Veterans, we appreciate all Veterans in all wars and peace.

3. Did you know that Veterans Day was originally called Armistice Day? Armistice Day was commemorating the end of World War I. When the Treaty of Versailles was signed on June 28, 1919, World War I officially ended. However, about seven months before that signing, the fighting ended. The fact is when the Allies and Germany put into effect an armistice on the eleventh hour of the eleventh day of the eleventh month. November 11, 1918 was considered the end of "the war to end all wars" and unofficially name Armistice Day. It officially became a holiday in 1938 at the end of the war. Therefore, a day was set aside to honor veterans of World War I. However, that is not the end. On June 1, 1954, after World War II and the Korean War, Congress amended the commemoration by changing the word "armistice" to "veterans" so the day would honor American veterans of ALL wars. But it didn't end there either. In 1968 Congress signed the "Uniform Holiday Bill" to ensure that a few federal holidays, including Veterans Day and Memorial Day, would be celebrated on a Monday. That's why today, Veterans Day, is observed on Monday, November 11th. However, it took three years for the new bill to be implemented on October 25, 1971.

SECTION SIX

POEM - Thank You for Your Sacrifice

Serving in the Vietnam War

WAS A SACRIFICE

Too many soldiers

Did not make it Back Home

Because they Lost their Lives

The Army, Navy, Air Force, and Marines

All were called

To SERVE our Country

OH, WHAT A SACRIFICE

FOR ALL HUMANITY

Veterans Day is Observed

TO SAY THANK YOU

But it seems there is More

That We Can Do

There shouldn't be any Vets HOMELESS

Or ANY Looking for Work

Due to their Sacrifice

They should have had the governments

FULL SUPPORT

They should have Felt Safe

As if, they were being held by

LOVING ARMS

But instead,

Many of them are SUFFERING from PTSD

Or long-term Health Issues

Due to the Chemical AGENT ORANGE!

Just imagine having to Shoot On Command

Not knowing whether again

You will see your Fellow Man

Not knowing all the Lives

You may have Taken

Not knowing when you go asleep

will you BE AWAKEN

And when you Return Home

There was NO COMPASSION

From Family and Friends

Instead, they were called

A Child Killer, Spit at and Robbed to No End

Some soldiers felt like they were

IN A WAR ALL OVER AGAIN

Most soldiers were in Survival Mode

And still had Flashbacks

Peace in their Minds

WILL THEY EVER FEEL THAT?

OH, WHAT A SACRIFICE

Our Soldiers did for us

All we can do is CONTINUOUSLY

PRAY for them

That they will be BLESSED

The entire Situation is Unfair

The returning Soldiers feel like

Americans and the Government

Let them down

AND WE DON'T CARE!

So think about ALL the Soldiers

That Lost their Lives

And THANK the ones that were Blessed

To Return home to Us

AND THANK THEM FOR

THEIR SACRIFICE

THE VISIONARY JEAN A. GLOVER - SCOTT

The visionary Jean A. Glover-Scott, also known as Jazzy Jean, is a Visionary who currently resides in Newark, Delaware. The Voices of Vietnam, Veterans Speaking Out, became her vision when she lost my husband to a fatal disease CJD (Creutzfeldt-Jakob Diseases). She wanted to give back to the Vietnam Veterans to let them know they haven't been forgotten and we appreciate their service. Jean is also the mother of five children (four gorgeous girls and one handsome son) and the Grandmother of eight beautiful grandchildren.

Jean has many gifts; she loves to write poetry and currently has two books written with her daughter Anelda aka Kitten. The titles are Poetry is Our Ministry and Our Ministry, His Words, The Continuation. One of her poems, titled Count Your Blessings, was nationally recognized. This both is also a collaboration with Anelda.

Jean's other passions are clothing designs and artwork. When she was in the sixth grade at George Washington Carver located at 1600 W. Norris Street in Philadelphia, PA, she started sketching and drawing. It was her teacher who discovered her gift of art. Then her teacher sent her to art school every Saturday. The school was located at 22nd Street and Columbia Avenue, which helped me to develop her gift.

When she attended Simon Gratz High School, her gift became stronger, and Jean developed the skills where she was able to draw students/teachers portraits just by sitting in front of her with ease. Her art teachers said that she was talented. Her artwork and portraits were displayed throughout the school.

Later, Jean and her family moved to Logan (above North Philadelphia), and she loved to dress her three girls alike. Anelda, Larenda, and Sharnika. She would make them pants and tops, which her neighbors always admired. Some people even thought her two youngest daughters Larenda and Sharnika, were twins. Thanks to Jean's gift and eye for fashion Anelda went on to win the title "Best Dress" for her graduating class.

Later, Jean had another daughter Marquita, and when she turned five, that's when my designing and creativity were on point. She started designing clothes and kept her dressed in sequins, rhinestones, and jackets with fringes and rhinestones. Her designs were featured in fashion shows.

From 1992 until 1994, Jean worked for the School Board of Philadelphia. She was still designing in her past time. Jean would design clothes for teachers, neighbors and continued designing for her children.

A few years later, Jean and her family moved to Delaware. This is where she started drawing clothing designs of formal dresses and elegant gowns, some with hats and shawls to match. Jazzy Jean is wearing her design in her photo. She even had a book of children's designs. Jean had over 300 designs in three books. At this point, only she and her late husband knew that Jean had these books of designs. It wasn't until her husband passed away that Jean decided to show all of her children her designs. They all agreed that they were beautiful and she should get them made.

A week later, my best friend Claudia Yancy and her husband Joe, brought her to Pilgrim Baptist Church, which she joined the first time she went. The church was a lifeline for her. They had a Grief Ministry and a Sewing Ministry.

During the Grief Ministry, she was able to let her feelings go and receive great support. When she found out that Pilgrim had a Sewing Ministry, Jean was excited and brought some of her book design sketches. Jean showed them to the seamstress Virginia Graves and they went to work on seven of them. At times, she would make small suggestions and add her input. They have made several dressed to date.

Coming to Pilgrim Baptist Church has been a blessing to her and a new lifeline. There are truly no words to express how grateful she feels. She loves Pastor Rector's preaching, the choirs singing, and, last but not least, Pastor Rector's beautiful wife, Sister Rector. Her encouragement brings her peace. She is honored to be a part of the Sheppard's Care Ministry. Also, anyone can tell you that Sister Jean A. Glover-Scott gets her Praise On! Most importantly, she feels stronger than she's ever been. She gives God the Glory for all that He has done.

At this time, the world is dealing with a pandemic due to COVID-19. Jean has put her gifts and talents to work again. She has designed beautiful masks with bling! Everyone loves them. We expect to see great things from this visionary

May God bless you all and Jean's desire that you share this book with any Vietnam Veteran, your family, and friends.

ABOUT THE AUTHOR

The author, Anelda L. Attaway, also known as Kitten and Jazzy Kitty, resides in New Castle, Delaware.

but was born in raised in Philadelphia in the "Logan Section." She was always an excellent student. She graduated with honors from Frankford High School in 1984.

Anelda is currently married and has one child. She is an Evangelist, book publisher of over 100 authors, an author, ghostwriter, editor, poet, and a Spoken Word artist. In addition to her writing gifts, she is an actress and a model for Jessie II Boutique.

Kitten, as her friends and family affectionately call her, loves to dance. She was one of the featured dancers on the hit dance reality show "Dancin' on Air" in the 80s. Dancin' On Air was produced at WPHL Channel 17 studios in Philadelphia, PA.

Anelda has been in many plays, most known for her role in King David as "Queen Vashti" and "The Bag Lady." Anelda received Christ as her Lord and Savior at a young age and became ordained as a Deacon and then an Evangelist in 2010. She uses her gift of poetry weekly to evangelize to the church congregation.

God gave Anelda, aka "Jazzy Kitty," a vision when she became very ill with the condition called the Shingles. God told her to "Pick up a pen and write." That is when she discovered her gift of writing poetry. Writing poetry, along with God's love and mercy, saved her life, and her body was healed.

Anelda was called to the ministry years ago and now is very excited about giving the testimony of her healing and spreading God's word. She wrote two books along with her mother called Poetry is Our Ministry "To touch the Heart" and Our Ministry, His Words written through the Holy Spirit to heal the Mind and Soul, most importantly to Save Souls. These books helped launch her business Jazzy Kitty Publishing in 2005.

She is currently the CEO of Jazzy Kitty Publications, formerly known as Jazzy Kitty Publishing, which provides inspiring self-publishing authors with the services they need to become published. They have published over 80 authors to date. Jazzy Kitty Publications also has a prison ministry that is dear to her heart. In the business world, she is known as "Jazzy Kitty," which is now a part of her brand.

She started her publishing company because she wanted everyone who dreams of becoming a published author dreams to come true!

Jazzy Kitty Publishing dba Jazzy Kitty Publishing is a Christian based publishing company. However, in the last five years, she has been affiliated with various genres, including urban fiction. She has been blessed with much favor from God through radio, Cable TV, newspaper write-ups, and more. She was invited to Phenix City, Alabama, and Atlanta to promote Jazzy Kitty Publications. She has been interviewed on Glory to God TV, WTMR 800 AM, Empowerment 4 U, to name a few. Her interviews can be heard on iTunes, iHeartRadio.com, and YouTube and viewed on Empowerment 4 U. Jazzy Kitty will be hosting her radio show called The Jazzy Kitty Show and TV show called Jazzy Kitty TV. These are to help promote her authors and entrepreneurs with a small business. She is currently the Media Specialist (Digital Newsletters and Social Media, to name a few for Power Up 4 Success, under the direction of Dr. Marci Bryant, the Founder.

Please see her website www.jazzykittypublications.com and blog to learn more about her and Jazzy Kitty Publications.

REFERENCES

These are the facts taken from these resources below:

- https://thevietnamwar.info
- Pilgrim Baptist Church Veterans Ministry
- https://www.publichealth.va.gov
- https://www.virtualwall.org
- https://www.history.com
- https://en.wikipedia.org/wiki/Agent_Orange
- https://www.defense.gov/Explore/Features/story/Article/1675470/5-facts-to-know-about-veterans-day/
- https://www.publichealth.va.gov/exposures/agentorange/benefits/registry-exam.asp

THANK YOU

FOR YOUR SERVICE!!!

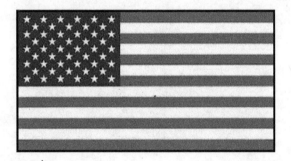

CPSIA information can be obtained
at www.ICGtesting.com
Printed in the USA
LVHW011138201120
672013LV00006B/1120

9 781735 787442